Midnight Rain

SAPPHIC POEMS

*for girls who are
brave enough
to love*

Dewdrops of Dawn

Midnight Rain by iris song

i know now that
i no longer want a half love

a sometimes there
and sometimes gone love

i want the kind of full hearted love
where you hold each other all night

and talk till the early hours
of a gentle misty morning

i want someone who truly sees me
and still wants to stay

    - *for keeps*

Midnight Rain by iris song

when you were little
someone gave you fairytales to read
and you fell in love with them
but now as an adult
they laugh at you for believing

don't listen to them
keep those enchanted stories alive
the sun still loves you
and the trees still whisper you secrets
make friends with the rabbits

and the frogs and all things
that once brought you joy
as a child, you are exactly
the kind of magic we need
in this world

don't give up
on the fairytale
that makes you
who you are

Midnight Rain by iris song

i spent so many years
afraid to love
only to realise
that love
had *already*
happened to me
it quietly crept into my dreams

she is all i have ever wanted
and all i ever dreamed of

Midnight Rain by iris song

you are every fairytale
i have ever read
come alive
in the best possible way

- *loving you is finding my childhood again*

Midnight Rain by iris song

i did what was asked of me
i dated who my parents wanted
because i needed their approval
and for them to love me

and then she came along,
with her beautiful eyes
and her joyous laugh
and taught me

    - *this is what love is supposed to feel like*

Midnight Rain by iris song

people keep trying to tell me
this kind of love is dirty
but this is the purest thing
that has ever happened to me
and she is the quiet gentle heaven
i have always imagined

Midnight Rain by iris song

if loving her
is so wrong
then i don't
ever want
to know
what is right

Midnight Rain by iris song

you have been
at rock bottom
so often before
because of a love
that wouldn't
love you back

you've forgotten
that a good love
won't leave you
on the floor
wounded and crying
all alone in your pain

Midnight Rain by iris song

i am so scared my parents
will find out about us
and find a way to destroy
this castle we have built together

Midnight Rain by iris song

far too many people leave
when you start to become
who you have always meant to be

your truth is not for the faint hearted
your love was not made for cowards
the ones who stay will show you

- *unconditional love*

Midnight Rain by iris song

i grew up in a place
where holding her hand
could ruin both our lives
so i know the courage
of simple gestures well
i know what its like
to put my life
on the line for love

   - *what brave looks like*

Midnight Rain by iris song

the thing is
he was comfortable to me
he knew how to make me smile
sweet sunshine boy
that everyone loved
so when everyone else said
i must love him back
i did as i was told

- *i confused comfort for love*

Midnight Rain by iris song

i made a list
of all the things
that made me happy

and titled it
with your name

Midnight Rain by iris song

i hope
i can love you
with the courage
you deserve

    - *fearless*

Midnight Rain by iris song

i don't even know
when it happened
but love came to me
quietly in all these little things you do,
the simple joy of your company
the way your hair falls into your eyes
how your eyes light up
when you talk about art
and music,

i couldn't help but wonder
how it would feel
to kiss you

Midnight Rain by iris song

you made every love song,
every poem, every piece of art
i ever heard and experienced
finally make sense

Midnight Rain by iris song

i've never believed anyone
when they told me i was beautiful
until you whispered it
against my lips

- *first kiss*

Midnight Rain by iris song

tell me every hope and dreams
you hid from everyone else
and i will tell you mine

lets build a universe
just for the two of us
right here in your bedroom

if forever ever existed
let it be this moment
let it be us, let it be this

Midnight Rain by iris song

the movies lie to us
when they say you'll come out
only once, just once,
this big event
and then its over.
your life is a series
of coming outs
your world is often changed
by the aftermath of each
time you come out
and you learn to survive
and thrive despite everything

    -   *and that is true courage*

Midnight Rain by iris song

QUEER JOY MATTERS.
QUEER JOY IS VALID.
QUEER LOVE IS LOVE.
QUEER HOPE IS WORTH
FIGHTING FOR.

Midnight Rain by iris song

I will battle everyone who tells me our love isn't worth it. That our love is somehow less because it doesn't look like what they were taught growing up. Every time she kisses me, I feel every storm cloud in my soul lift, she brings in peace where there is tragedy, our love is the gentlest God I know, raising us up together so we can touch the sky.

- *our love was made different*

Midnight Rain by iris song

loving you has taught me that i am more water than fire, how people like us are the ocean's song, the stories whispered by every tree to the wind, how love is older and more ancient than anything that has tried to destroy it and it has always won. It is still here despite every odd, just like our love will be.

- *we were here and we loved*

Midnight Rain by iris song

in an alternate universe,
we stand on bridges and kiss
till the sun goes down
and we practice small joys together
and know that when we promise
each other a life time,
it really does mean
a possible forever

- *a place we dream of*

Midnight Rain by iris song

to put my arm around her
in front of my parents
is the most terrifying
and exhilarating thing
i ever did.

Midnight Rain by iris song

thank you for showing me
how sacred love can be,
how divine our bodies are
when we lie together
naked and counting the stars.

- *the night we were immortal*

Midnight Rain by iris song

it was the deep conversations
and the gentle, quiet connections,
the way we loved all the same songs
and the way we talked to each other
like we put the moon in the sky
and then painted countless stars
around her, just to give her company.

- *falling in love with you*

Midnight Rain by iris song

i assumed i was hard to love
difficult to have around
too strange to know
let alone hold,
it took me some time
to realise
that i was easy to love,
i just needed
to find someone
who had a heart
as gentle and strange
as mine.

Midnight Rain by iris song

i am learning to reject everything
that tells me i am gross or wrong
or misguided or bad
for being gay
for loving you
this deeply
and in this
powerful way

- *you make me the best version of myself*

Midnight Rain by iris song

you were the soft voice
i desperately needed
after a lifetime
of harsh sharp edged voices.

you were the gentle hand
that soothed my furrowed brow
and whispered peace into my ear
when i nearly have up.

i have a lot to thank you for
but thank you most of all
for being the calm i needed
when i needed it the most

    -   *i am so honoured to be loved so kindly by you*

Midnight Rain by iris song

the most beautiful flowers
rain after the most brutal storms

- *things you taught me*

Midnight Rain by iris song

who am i without
the pain
the sadness
the fear
the noise
the noise
the noise in my head

and you take my hand
and tell me
you are the best thing
that ever happened to me
a fairytale
i carry within my soul

Midnight Rain by iris song

there is a version of me
out there somewhere
who has never known pain
and trauma and self hatred
since she was a child.
i hope she got the boring
carefree childhood I wished for
when i was growing up
i hope she never knows pain
the way i was forced to

- *wishes for another universe 1*

Midnight Rain by iris song

it shouldn't be so hard
to be happy in a relationship.
it shouldn't be so hard
to love someone back.

   -   *why i left him*

Midnight Rain by iris song

if i picture my life ten years from now, i picture myself at a wooden kitchen table drinking a cup of hot tea. outside the mist swivels through the quiet forest just beyond my garden. i have so many books to keep me company, a hundred adventures yet to go on. i picture a little life, peaceful and free.

Midnight Rain by iris song

to be here
and to be alive
despite all the pain
despite all these scars
and to still be loved by you
is the greatest gift
the universe has ever
given me.

    - *gratitude*

Midnight Rain by iris song

Truthfully, I think in some ways it was our sadness that brought us together. The fact that neither of us fit into this world that demanded we act a certain way to be loved, even by our own parents. It feels like the only place we can be honest is with each other. The only peace is what we have made together.

Midnight Rain by iris song

i had to leave him
because i couldn't be
what he wanted me to be
and what I wanted to be
at the same time

Midnight Rain by iris song

i have this theory
that somewhere in another universe
a different earth exists
where no mothers tell us
we are sinful
and no fathers look away in disgust
no small town judgement comes our way
as we walk together down
a cobble stone street
and we kiss right there
in the middle of town
and the sun glitters on us
and blesses us as holy.

Midnight Rain by iris song

Did I ever love him or was I just pretending to make him happy. Did I ever love him or was I just pretending to make him happy.

…do I even like boys?

Midnight Rain by iris song

does she love me back
the way I love her?
or am i an experiment
and not a forever?

    -   *lavender crisis*

Twilight Storm

Midnight Rain by iris song

if my parents can't accept me
no matter who i love
then did they ever
truly love me unconditionally
at all?

> - *children do not exist simply to reinforce your toxic worldview*

Midnight Rain by iris song

believe me when i say this
all these tears you're crying are not lost
and the love you have given to someone
is never ever lost,
because you have always loved hard
so hard that they will look for you
in everyone, carry pieces
of the love you gave them
everywhere they go
they will remember one day
how deeply you have cared for them
and even if they don't admit it
and don't look like they are
they will always know
the absence of your
deep powerful love

    - *to love deeply is a gift not a curse*

Midnight Rain by iris song

loving you has been
the best and easiest thing
i have ever done.

i hope i can show you
that you are not hard to love
and heal some of the hurt

others caused you
by making you feel
like loving you is hard work.

- *its not you its them*

Midnight Rain by iris song

i think i realised that I was in love
with you when a good thing happened to me
and you were the first person i called
because yours was the only voice
i wanted to hear

    -   *a realisation*

Midnight Rain by iris song

a series of what ifs that will heal instead of hurt

what if she loves you back?
what if it all works out in the end?
what if it not working out means you'll be happier?
what if your heartbreak heals?
what if you make it through it all?
what if it ends and it doesn't hurt?
what if all this pain is necessary lessons?
What if you heal instead of hurt?

Midnight Rain by iris song

hurricanes and quiet girls
have so much in common.
no one sees them coming
or understand the full magnitude
of what they carry inside them.

Midnight Rain by iris song

i can't stop thinking about how we almost never happened. if i had walked into that café five minutes too late, i would have never bumped into you and you would have never spilled your coffee, and i would never have bought you a second one and you would have never smiled and asked me to meet you again sometime so you could return the favour. i have never used to believe the universe works in mysterious ways, but no one can ever tell me that the universe wasn't conspiring for us to meet.

- *tell me this isn't fate*

Midnight Rain by iris song

i wish i wasn't so afraid
to be my real self
in front of my parents
but i remember how my mother
looked at those two girls
kissing on the television screen,
like they were disgusting.
i am scared she will look at me
the same way.
i am scared she will never
stop looking at me that way
ever again.

- *how do i tell her who i am*

Midnight Rain by iris song

i feel like i am suffocating
pretending to be a person i am not,
just to make my parents happy
just to hear them say
how proud they are of me.

Midnight Rain by iris song

is it possible for a parent
to stop loving a child
because of who that child loves?

- *questions for a god i no longer believe in*

Midnight Rain by iris song

if my parents are hurt
by something i cannot help being
is that still my fault?

- *questions for a god i no longer believe in 2*

Midnight Rain by iris song

i am trying to make myself brave by reminding myself that the approval of my parents isn't a requirement. it isn't essential for my being. i can live without their love if i have to, find my own family instead, build another one where i can be entirely me and be loved exactly as who i am, somewhere i can be free.

- *if i have to grow beyond my parents, i will*

Midnight Rain by iris song

i had come to accept loneliness
as a friend, the silence as self control.
i taught myself all this
was better than a broken heart

this is why when you first appeared
in my life i was so scared to love you,
because it would mean admitting
that i needed you more

than the alone
i had become
so used to.

but the truth is
i do need you
more than anything in the world
you are the only person

i have ever needed in my life.

Midnight Rain by iris song

there are so many people
who will love you
for who you are
than who you are
pretending to be

- *found families exist*

Midnight Rain by iris song

if your love is so easy
to snatch back
then we don't want it

- *to parents who disown their queer kids*

Midnight Rain by iris song

i hope the way you treated me
haunts you every night.
i hope i am the only portrait
in your haunted house of guilt.

Midnight Rain by iris song

if i am not allowed to love her this way,
this passionate
all consuming,
intensely powerful way
then I refuse to love ever again.

- *what i told my mother*

Midnight Rain by iris song

i didn't know being your daughter
came with terms and conditions
i don't remember signing a contract
that said if i am not perfect,
i am not worthy of your love.

- *what i said to my father*

Midnight Rain by iris song

i'm sorry for all the times i said I love you,
i do love you just not that way,
i can never love a man the way
i love a woman
i should have been brave enough
to be honest with you
from the start

- *what i told him when we broke up*

Midnight Rain by iris song

i have never felt more lonely
than after i came out to everyone
who was supposed to love me.

   - *but my god, i have never felt more alive*

Midnight Rain by iris song

all these tears you are crying
are falling upon seeds that
will one day grow into
radiant flowers
i promise i promise i promise

Midnight Rain by iris song

the seconds after you burn it all down,
where you destroy the old version of you
where you shatter the illusion
you have built for those you love
there is fear
there is rejection
but there is also *freedom*

Midnight Rain by iris song

you are not less worthy of love
because someone
who should have loved you
did not love you
the way you deserved

- *lesson learned*

Midnight Rain by iris song

they want to hurt us
because we are braver
than they could ever be,
because we are living
more honestly
than they can ever try,
because we scare them,
we scare them,
we show them every day
what it is like to live
truly fearlessly.

- *a brief note on homophobes*

Midnight Rain by iris song

sometimes the person you love is just a figment of your imagination because the person you love existed behind a mask. once you see the mask fall away, you recognise that you've been building dreams around someone that never existed and the grief of this is what breaks us and wrecks our hearts.

Midnight Rain by iris song

sometimes the universe
says no.
not because you don't deserve
the thing you want so badly
but because it is saving you
from the pain
of what may happen
after you receive it.

- *lessons learned 2*

Midnight Rain by iris song

Some questions
are easier to answer
than others.

"Do you love me?"

should have been easy
for you to answer
if you ever truly did.

Instead you met it
with silence.

Which it turns out
is also an answer.

Midnight Rain by iris song

we spend so much time
apologising
to people who leave
without realising that
we were the ones
who cared enough
to stay and work things out.

- *lessons learned 3*

Midnight Rain by iris song

when the time comes
i hope we can
let each other go
with grace and kindness
rather than anger and despair

- *on endings*

Midnight Rain by iris song

my parents
treat my brother's girlfriend
like she is family
and treat mine
like she is a ghost
they cannot even see

Midnight Rain by iris song

one day
you will meet someone
who is the beautiful story
that the gods wrote
just to help you survive

Midnight Rain by iris song

please don't give up. if they don't love you, there is still hope. if your family rejects you, there are people you haven't met yet who will love you. it may sound cliché but the world has need of you, your spirit, your joy because there is no one else in the world quite like you. the universe placed you right here in this life for a reason. i promise you will survive this. you *will* survive this.

- *thank you for being here*

Midnight Rain by iris song

your trauma doesn't define your strength,
you were already strong when it happened to you.
how else do you think you survived it
if not for the fire already burning within you.

Midnight Rain by iris song

you will be okay.
even after this.
it may take some time.
and things may hurt for a while.
but you will heal
and you will be okay.

   -   *eventually all wounds become scars*

Midnight Rain by iris song

i love her in every possible, audacious, maddening way. i love her despite all the discouragement from those around us, i love her through her sadness and mine, i love her in peace and in fury, in prayer and in promise, in fire and brimstone and nothing anyone can say will ever change that

- *if the gods themselves demand i stop, i will defy them*

Midnight Rain by iris song

my grandfather held my grandmother like she was a bird. gently enough so that she could choose to fly away any time she chose. tenderly enough so she knew his love was always there to nourish her. in return, my grandmother loved my grandfather the way an ocean loves the shore. always returning, never forgetting what love is for. that taught me so much about love. they taught me so much about love.

Midnight Rain

Midnight Rain by iris song

"What's on your mind?"

"You. Always and constantly, you."

Midnight Rain by iris song

you are the most delightfully sinful thing
that has ever happened to me.
all crimson apple sweetness.
all emerald absinthe wicked.

- *fairytale love*

Midnight Rain by iris song

every time i am with you,
i feel the world disappear
and all those problems
i had seem so small.
loving you is the only thing
that makes me feel
like I belong here.
like you are home.

- *this is how love heals*

Midnight Rain by iris song

i just want someone
who will promise me
that we will wake up
every morning together
and that is what the universe
gives us in the end.

- *a promise*

Midnight Rain by iris song

there is not a lot i hope for
but in the end, in the very end
i hope it's us.
i hope it's us against everything.
i know i can take on the whole world
as long as we do it together
holding hands.

Midnight Rain by iris song

i knew i loved you
when i left the last piece
of my favourite cake for you
and the first time i saw
a vibrant blue butterfly
the only person i shared
my awe with was you
and when i finally,
finally managed to run
across that finish line,
the only face i looked for
was yours.

in a sea of people,
the only person i ever
search for
is you.

Midnight Rain by iris song

there is still so much to learn
about this world.
more books to read
and art to see
and souls to start
late night conversations with
and fall in love with
if nothing else,
i'll stay to watch
the flowers come out
next spring

- *things to stay for*

Midnight Rain by iris song

i know
i have loved you
more clearly
more beautifully
than anyone else
every part of you
is precious to me
every time you speak
of all the things you love
you glow so brightly.

Midnight Rain by iris song

we have loved each other
in a thousand lifetimes
of this i am sure

i know it from the way
my soul recognises yours.

- *our love is ancient*

Midnight Rain by iris song

please don't let this be a temporary love. please don't let this be a temporary love. please don't let this be a temporary love like all the others before it, let this last, let this last, let this last.

- *a prayer*

Midnight Rain by iris song

this is for the loud girls and the screaming girls and the girls who are too bright for this world and hold so much anger and pain inside them that they do not fit in. this is for the girls who know darkness better than they have known light and whose parents tried to turn them into something they are not but never succeeded. girls who are told they are dangerous and girls who are told they are mad for wanting so much, so very much from a world that is terrified of them.

i promise you, love is coming for you just as you are.

- *hold on*

Midnight Rain by iris song

she made me fall in such a way
that i found myself in the ashes
of who i used to be.

i know now that
her body and mine
were made to be each other's home.

she is
the safest place
i have ever known.

Midnight Rain by iris song

what else do two girls
who love the rain
and mist and books
and dark stormy days
have in common?

it turns out
all the love
in the whole
wide world.

Midnight Rain by iris song

i am trying to pretend
that losing you doesn't feel
like the sun losing the moon
and being asked to rise
every morning
and shine as brightly
while knowing she is no longer there.

- *losing you may not destroy me but it will take what natters from my soul*

Midnight Rain by iris song

growing up queer
means learning to tune the world out
when it constantly tells you
that you shouldn't exist
and learning to be proud
of who you are despite
its best efforts to crush your spirit

Midnight Rain by iris song

queer children do not owe you
explanations as to why we are queer
if your love is unconditional for your child
you wouldn't need an explanation anyway

>   - *if you cannot handle having a queer child, do not have children*

Midnight Rain by iris song

to be this deeply in love is a joy
to know my heart can be broken
by someone as beautiful as you is a privilege
you are the risk i always thought worth taking
to be loved by you in any capacity
is an honour i never thought i would have

thank you for healing me in ways
i never thought I could heal myself

Midnight Rain by iris song

the thing isn't just that you survived it.
the thing is that you lived past the pain
the trauma, the sadness,
everything that nearly
destroyed you

and you fought so hard
that it gave up

Midnight Rain by iris song

yes it *was* that bad.
stop gaslighting yourself.
if you're still thinking about it
and still trying to heal from it
then yes it was that bad.

- *you must acknowledge the pain to heal from it*

Midnight Rain by iris song

the truth is,
even if you left tomorrow
ghosted me
or simply told me
you couldn't be
with me anymore
despite all the pain
i will still choose you
even after a thousand lifetimes
i would still choose you

Midnight Rain by iris song

if you ever find a person
that looks at you
like you painted the stars
into a midnight sky,
love them ceaselessly,
endlessly, the way the stars
adore the darkness
which gives them a home
in which to shine

- *i hope someone looks at you that way*

Midnight Rain by iris song

if the people you love tell you that you cannot be loved as who you are, know that they do not deserve to know you in your freedom.

the most cruel unkind people are that way because they are unhappy and cannot stand to see joy on anyone else.

you cannot change the way the world responds to you but you can change the way you respond to it.

if you allow yourself to love deeply, you will find the strength you have always been seeking.

your love is the antidote, it is not the poison.

- *5 lessons i learned from finally being myself*

Midnight Rain by iris song

"so this is it. this is what it has all been about."

"what?"

"you."

"what about me?"

"you are it. you are everything i could have hoped for in human form.."

- *a place of peace*

Midnight Rain by iris song

the devastation in always feeling
so very deeply all the time
is that you cannot make others
feel as deeply as you do.
this is why you feel so lonely.
because you know and love the world
better than it knows and loves you.

Midnight Rain by iris song

is there anything better
than falling asleep
to the sound
of your lover's steady heartbeat
while the rain gently dances
on your window?

Midnight Rain by iris song

i hope to give the people
i come across the comfort
i wish i had when i was scared,
in pain, lost.

before i leave this earth,
i hope i can be a safe place for
someone who needs it most of all.
a home for outcasts like me.

Midnight Rain by iris song

i don't know how to explain to people that I feel uncomfortable in my body. not overweight, not underweight, not ugly or pretty, not any of those descriptions people use, just…uncomfortable. I feel like no label anyone uses to describe themselves can be used to describe me, i just want to leap out of my body one day and feel alive. there must be a way, right? to breathe and exist and feel truly free?

Midnight Rain by iris song

if my family loves me less
for being myself
after a lifetime of
teaching me
to be honest,
then they are
the cruel ones
not me.

- *If your family cannot handle your truth, you deserve better*

Midnight Rain by iris song

think about this:
if there is a God,
an omniscient being
that never makes mistakes
that is *always* right
without exception,
then how could you be wrong,
how could who you love
possibly be a mistake?

- *on religious guilt*

Midnight Rain by iris song

people will love you
and still end up treating you poorly.
not because they want to
but because they are hurt themselves
or don't know how to show you they love you
or they show you they love you,
feel afraid and withdraw that love.
the way they treat you
is not a reflection of you.
it is a reflection of who *they* are.

- *the people who hurt you do not define you*

Midnight Rain by iris song

you are the reason why
my world finally makes sense.
i'm afraid that if you leave,
everything will stop making sense again.

- *attachment theory*

Midnight Rain by iris song

if we do not last,
if the forevers we promised each other
end up being forgotten and temporary,
i want you to know that no matter what
you will always be loved
and have a home right here
with me

Midnight Rain by iris song

if no one has told you this today:
you are important, valued and loved.
you are needed.
you will find what you are looking for
in the most quiet unexpected places.
you deserve joy and goodness
and kindness in your life.

- *yes you are worthy*

Midnight Rain by iris song

can i tell you a secret?

even the worst version of you deserves love.
especially when you don't believe
you are worthy of it.
you must learn to love the part of yourself
no one has ever loved to heal.

Midnight Rain by iris song

you must ask yourself what truly makes you happy. what version of you feels most comfortable. what part of you feels like the truth and which parts of you are the lie you are inventing for others. and once you find it, once you find that honest version of yourself, hold onto that. your joy was not made to be a small, hidden thing in the dark, it was meant to gleam like a jewel out in the sun. find your joy and don't let anyone ever take that away. because in the end, that's all that matters anyway, the world is a better place when people are happy because joy is infectious.

Midnight Rain by iris song

i would rather have
my heart broken a thousand more times
than go back into the closet again.
i would rather be nobody
than be anything other than
my whole self.

- *and no one can take that away from me*

Midnight Rain by iris song

Picture yourself as a child and say: it's okay to make mistakes. You are still loved. It's okay to be loud and angry sometimes. You are still loved. It's okay to escape into your imagination when things get hard. You are still loved. Yes you can cry as much as you need. You will always be loved I'm so proud of you for being strong enough to stay here. I hope I can do everything I can to make you feel safe and loved.

- *inner child healing*

Midnight Rain by iris song

bless the girls we used to be
that became the women
we are today all fearless and free
and angry and still fighting.

- *survival is never pretty but here we are*

Midnight Rain by iris song

i hope we all find the love,
hope and peace
we have been seeking
our whole lives.

and when we find it
may we accept it
with open hearts
and smiles and joy

Thank you so much for reading! If you could please review the book, I would deeply appreciate it, thank you for supporting this little book!

About the author

Iris Song is a poet who lives inside a forest. She loves misty mornings, steamy cups of tea and the moon. She still believes in love and hope.

Printed in Great Britain
by Amazon